College Hacks
(kä-lij, haks) noun.

Keith Bradford

Adams Media
New York London Toronto Sydney New Delhi

Adams Media
An Imprint of Simon & Schuster, Inc.
57 Littlefield Street
Avon, Massachusetts 02322

For information about special discounts for bulk purchases, please contact Simon & Schuster Special Sales at 1-866-506-1949 or business@simonandschuster.com.

The Simon & Schuster Speakers Bureau can bring authors to your live event. For more information or to book an event contact the Simon & Schuster Speakers Bureau at 1-866-248-3049 or visit our website at www.simonspeakers.com.

Interior illustrations by Kathy Konkle © Simon & Schuster, Inc.

Manufactured in the United States of America

10 9 8 7

Library of Congress Cataloging-in-Publication Data has been applied for.

ISBN 978-1-4405-9004-7
ISBN 978-1-4405-9005-4 (ebook)

Contents

Introduction

Welcome to the college life, where the parties are wilder, the tests are harder, and you're lucky if your teacher only assigns you a 20-page paper. Sure, you could go through the next few years in a stressed-out flock of college students, scraping by from one exam to the next, but why work so hard when you don't have to? In this indispensible guide, you'll find simple solutions to scenarios you're guaranteed to face at some point in your college career. From quickly coming up with a bibliography (even though you only used one Wikipedia page) to mastering the art of beer pong, each page will teach you how to get any task done easily and more quickly and efficiently than you would have before.

The majority of these college hacks have been pulled from various sources around the Internet as well as from user submissions to my blog 1000LifeHacks.com. I've broken the book down into ten different aspects of the college life, but you don't need to read them in chronological order; you can literally flip to any page and start improving your college life right now!

So stop making things a heck of a lot harder than they should be! With these everyday college hacks, you'll go from Joe Schmo to college student 2.0, and breeze through each semester without even breaking a sweat!

CHAPTER 1

Technology

On your first day of school, take a picture of your schedule and set it as your lock screen on your phone, so you always have it handy.

If you're having trouble with a math problem, plug the equation into *www.WolframAlpha.com* and it will solve it for you.

Confused by a Wikipedia article? Click "Simple English" on the left list of languages and it'll whisk you to a simplified version.

Need to test a printer? Print the Google homepage. It has all the colors you need to run a proper test, and it won't use a lot of ink.

Make sure you have at least one professional-sounding e-mail address. Nothing will turn off your teacher or future employer faster than *yoloswag420@bromail.com.*

Before you throw away a Post-it note, run it
sticky side down between the keys on your
keyboard to collect dust, crumbs, and other
things that might have gotten trapped in there.

When writing an e-mail, make sure the last thing you do is put in the recipient's e-mail address. This will help you avoid sending an unfinished e-mail.

Studying for an important test? Google "site:edu (subject) exam". You'll get a bunch of different college exams with problems similar to what may be on your test.

10 Search Operators to Help You Search Google Like a Pro

1   **ASTERISK**
Searches for a missing word in phrase.
Example: Obama was president for * years

2   **SITE:**
Only shows search results from a specific website.
Example: site:1000lifehacks.com

3   **TWO PERIODS**
Searches between two specific numbers.
Example: Number 1 movies between 1980..1990

4   **VERTICAL BAR**
Searches for sites that have one/two/all terms.
Example: blouse | shirt | chemise

5   **OR**
Search with multiple synonyms to get more specific results.
Example: Literacy OR Learning

6 **% OF**
Instantly get the percentage of any number.
Example: 12% of 75

7 **FILETYPE:**
Search for a specific type of file.
Example: Declaration of Independence filetype:pdf

8 **DASHES**
Excludes a certain word from your search.
Example: Homer -Simpson

9 **QUOTATION MARKS**
Searches for exact the words, quotes, or phrases you're looking for.
Example: "I have a dream"

10 **DEFINE:**
Gets a quick definition of a word.
Example: define: perplexed

When you copy something from the Internet, use "Ctrl + Shift + V" to paste it into a document. This will prevent the text from formatting.

Use your own original gifs in presentations by adding "gif" before the word "youtube" in the URL. Doing this allows you to create your own gif using the video.

You can press "1," "2," "3," etc. to jump 10%, 20%, 30% into the video you're watching on YouTube.

Forget slow double clicks! Press "F2" on a PC and "Enter/Return" on a Mac to immediately rename a file.

Need specific date ranges for a project? You can search "(month)(year)" in Wikipedia to give you all the major world news for that month.

If you're on a school computer that blocks sites like YouTube, Google Chrome's incognito mode will let you access them.

Hold down "Alt" and click on any Google image to have it automatically saved to your computer.

The iPhone app Scholly shows you thousands of potential scholarship opportunities that any student can apply for.

www.Mathway.com solves all kinds of math homework problems with step-by-step explanations.

Get the best possible sound from your iTunes by replicating these presets on the Equalizer.

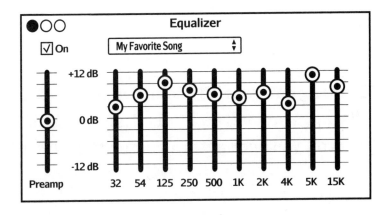

Need your phone's battery to make it to the end of class? Turning the flash off on your cell phone camera can extend your battery life even when you're not actually using the camera!

Cleaning out your Windows computer? Search "size:gigantic" and it'll display all the files on your computer greater than 128 MB.

You can amplify the sound on your computer
by cutting a plastic cup vertically in half
and placing each half over a speaker.

Want to make sure you get up in the morning
for class? The Snooze app for iPhone will
donate some of your money to charity each
time you hit the snooze button.

Need to cite a quote from a book? Don't bother looking through every page to find it! Simply type the quote into Google Books and it will tell you the page number automatically.

Forgot about an assignment and need to e-mail it? Change the date on your computer system before sending it to your professor.

Accidentally close a tab in your Internet browser? Press "Ctrl + Shift + T" to reopen it.

Need to edit an image quickly? On SumoPaint.com you can use an online version of Photoshop for free.

If you talk into the microphone instead of typing in Snapchat, you can send longer messages to your friends.

By charging your laptop battery only up to 80% instead of 100%, you can greatly extend the usable lifespan of the battery.

Too many Internet tabs open while doing homework? Simply right click on it and select "pin tab." Boom! Way more organized.

An iPad charger will charge your iPhone much faster.

How to boost the Wi-Fi in your dorm room:

1   Place an **X-Acto** knife just below the top rim of a beer or soda can and carefully cut through the can.

2   Now, place the knife just above the bottom rim of the can and cut through.

3   Using scissors, cut the aluminum in half vertically.

4   Spread the aluminum around your Wi-Fi antenna so that it forms a half circle around it.

Need to quickly solve a math problem?
The PhotoMath app will solve it by simply
pointing your phone's camera at the problem.

Need some Wi-Fi to finish a paper last
minute? You can get the Wi-Fi password to
almost anywhere by checking the comments
section on Foursquare.

Your headphones can be used as microphones if you plug them into the mic jack on your computer. This is helpful when recording lectures.

Want to know random trivia like a *Jeopardy!* champion? Set your homepage to Wikipedia's Random Article button. You'll learn something new every time you open a browser window.

Can't afford Microsoft Word? Get OpenOffice. It's the same thing except it's free and has a lot more features.

On a Mac, the easiest way to use special characters, like those weird accented "e"s, is to hold down the letter until a small menu pops up, then hit the corresponding number.

To resize a photo for Instagram, tilt your phone sideways and screenshot it. It'll fit perfectly without affecting the quality.

Forgot your computer password? Boot up in safe mode (F8 during startup), log in as the administrator, and then change your password.

10 Sites Every College Kid Should Bookmark

1 *www.RainyMood.com* is a website that makes it sound like it's raining outside. It's amazing if you need to concentrate on studying or getting work done.

2 *www.WordHippo.com* is a website that will help you find the word you're looking for when you can only think of a phrase to describe it.

3 On *www.PrintWhatYouLike.com* you can select exactly what you want to print from a desired webpage. No more printing ads, navigation bars, or weird comment boxes, just the essentials.

4 iRuler.net gives you an actual-sized virtual ruler if you don't have one on hand and need to measure something.

5 Lozo.com will give you coupons for each item on your shopping list.

6   On *www.PaperBackSwap.com* you can swap your old
books with other people online. You'll never have to
buy another book again!

7   MyFridgeFood.com will tell you everything you can
make with the items from your fridge.

8   Spreeder.com is a free online speed reading
software designed to improve your reading speed and
comprehension.

9   PizzaCodes.com is a site that gives you a list of promo
codes you can use to get a discount on pizza from most
pizza places.

10   On *www.Surfly.com* you can screen share your computer
with someone for free, which is perfect for study
sessions or having movie nights with your friends
back home.

If you lost an Android phone in your dorm room and it's on vibrate, you can find it by logging in to Android Device Manager online and clicking "ring."

Don't want your personal data all over the Internet? On *www.AccountKiller.com* you can remove it from a whole bunch of old and unwanted sites at once.

You can swipe left or right on the iPhone calculator to delete the last digit, so you don't have to start all over.

Keep your charger cord from bending or breaking by sliding it into a spring from an old pen.

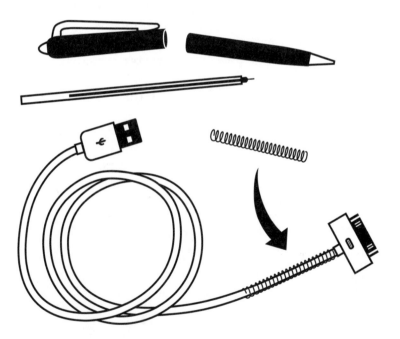

The Technology Checklist

- ☐ Computer or laptop

- ☐ Keyboard (if you have a computer)

- ☐ Mouse

- ☐ Ethernet cable

- ☐ Headphones

- ☐ External speakers

- ☐ Printer

- ☐ Printer ink and extra printer ink

- ☐ Printer paper

- ☐ USB flash drive

- ☐ HDMI cord

- ☐ Power bars

- ☐ TV

- ☐ Phone charger

CHAPTER 2

In the Classroom

Have a separate user account on your laptop for presentations. This way, embarrassing personal things won't show up on the screen when you turn it on in class.

Writing down your worries before taking an exam has been proven to actually boost your test scores.

Have a class or field trip somewhere outside?
Take vitamin B complex beforehand. Insects
don't like the way it makes you smell to them,
so it wards off mosquitoes and biting flies.

Sick of giving all your gum away to your
classmates? Keep two packs on you. One pack
full of gum and an empty pack to show people
you don't have any.

How to use your cell phone in class: Wear a long-sleeve hoodie to class and leave an empty sleeve on your desk. Snake your free arm underneath your hoodie and use that hand to text underneath your desk.

Stumped on a project or presentation? Try ditching the computer and start writing by hand. The experience has been proven to help creativity.

Get a paper cut in class? You can immediately stop the pain by rubbing ChapStick on the wounded area.

In the first few weeks of school, avoid people who want to be best friends right away. They're usually the overdramatic ones.

The best way to learn how to study for an exam is to ask your professors how they would study for their own exams.

If you accidentally get ink on your clothes, spray hairspray on the stain and it'll come right off.

10 Ways to Instantly De-stress in the Classroom

1   Take a few deep breaths. It seems obvious, but a few simple breaths can play a big part in nourishing your body—just ask anyone who does yoga.

2   Smile. Smiling, even when you're not happy, releases endorphins, the body's natural happy drug.

3   Stop staring at your computer screen. Uninterrupted computer use has been associated with stress. Try the rule of 20: Every 20 minutes look at something 20 feet away for 20 seconds.

4   Smell some lavender. Whether it's the plant or a scented candle, the scent of lavender has been known to calm, energize, and revitalize us.

5   Go to your happy place. Just like in *Happy Gilmore*, closing your eyes and visualizing yourself in a calm happy place can de-stress you within seconds.

6   Eat something. Stress is a brain and immune system mediated phenomenon, and your gut is the largest organ in your immune system, so eating will send a signal to your brain to calm down.

7   Try the Naam Yoga Hand Trick. Apply pressure to the space between your second and third knuckle (the joints at the base of your pointer and middle fingers). This can help create a sense of instant calmness.

8   Go to DoNothingFor2Minutes.com. This site encourages you to listen to relaxing ocean sounds without touching your mouse or keyboard.

9   Stretch. Stand up and do some arm, neck, and chest stretches to get your blood flowing. Good blood circulation is key to making your body feel good. Why do you think cats and dogs are always doing it?

10 Watch a funny video. By laughing at a funny video, your body increases its intake of oxygen-rich air, stimulates your heart, and increases the endorphins that are released by your brain. Who knew Keyboard Cat could do all that?

You can make your handwriting neater by using a lighter grip on your pen or pencil.

If you're giving a big presentation, have a friend ask you a set question. This way, you can come up with a great answer beforehand and it will look like you really know your stuff.

No ruler around? Improvise with a dollar bill. It's roughly 6 inches long.

You are more likely to remember something that you've written in blue ink than something you've written in black ink.

Did you step on some gum on the way to class?
Drop by the janitor closet and spray it with
WD-40. It will come right off!

If you drink enough fluids in the morning,
you'll feel happier, sharper, and more
energetic throughout the entirety of the
school day.

If you need to get stuff done and don't want anyone to bother you, wear headphones even if you're not listening to music.

Late for class and need to tell your professor a believable lie? Include an embarrassing detail about yourself. Nobody will doubt a story that makes you look dumb.

Get the sudden urge to pee in the middle of an exam? Thinking about sex will temporarily relieve the urge to pee and give you some extra time to finish your exam.

When proofreading something, read the document out loud to yourself. Your mouth will catch errors your mind might glance over.

Don't ask the teacher a question with 30 seconds left in class. People want to leave. Simply wait and approach him or her with the question after class is dismissed.

Keep pen thieves away: Put a blue ink cartridge in a red pen. No one steals red pens.

If you're struggling to remember a word, clench your fist. This increases brain activity and improves memory, making it easier for you to remember.

Need to cross out a word and don't want it to be legible? Don't scribble over it; instead write random letters and words over the original.

Taking a quick nap after learning something new can solidify that memory in your brain. Just make sure your professor doesn't catch you!

If your stomach is rumbling in class, do not clench your muscles; instead push your stomach out like a beer belly and the noise will stop.

Challenge yourself to find some fun in learning something new. This will make class interesting no matter how boring or stressful the day is.

When trying to figure out percentages (for example, 40% of 300) drop the last digit of the number and multiply by the 10s digit of the percent, so in this case, 4 × 30 = 120.

Want to remember your notes more easily?
Use a weird font style. Studies have shown
the uniqueness of a font will make you more
likely to remember what's written.

If a website is blocked on your school's
Internet, you can use Google Translate as a
proxy. Just copy and paste the URL into it.

Get a bad case of anxiety in class? Try this acupressure technique for instant anxiety relief. Just place three fingers right below your palm to measure out where your thumb should go and gently press down in the middle of where you place your third finger.

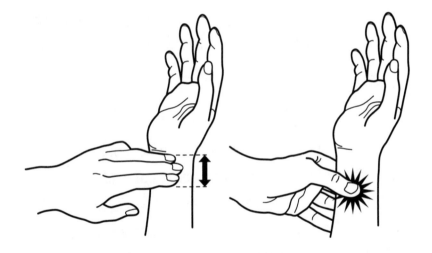

Study your notes within one day of taking them. Retention rates are 60% higher then.

Quickly convert kgs to lbs:
First, take the kgs and multiply them by 2.
Then take that number and divide it by 10.
Last, add the two numbers up.
For example: 100 kgs = 200 + 20 = 220 lbs.

If your calculator runs out of batteries in the middle of an exam, rub their ends together. This can give you up to an extra 15 minutes of battery life.

SelfControl is a program that blocks sites like Facebook, Twitter, and e-mail for a specified period of time. Using it will help you minimize distractions while in the classroom.

When doing a presentation in PowerPoint, always save it as a "PowerPoint Show" (.ppsx). This will open it directly to the slideshow.

Prevent your Apple earbuds from tangling when you're not using them by magnetically attaching them to the edges of your MacBook screen.

Feeling nervous about a presentation or exam? Start chewing gum. This tricks your brain into thinking that you're not in danger, because if you were, you would not be eating.

If you forget a classmate's name simply say, "Sorry, what was your name again?" They may look annoyed, but once they tell you their first name say, "No, I meant your last name."

It's actually better to take exams on an empty stomach. Hunger makes you focus better.

Stop using Google.com to search information for school essays.
Use scholar.google.com instead. You'll find more relevant information right away.

Writing your notes down with red ink on yellow paper will help you remember them.

Got a headache in class? Biting down on your pencil can get rid of it.

10 Classroom Etiquettes to Help You Stay on Your Teacher's Good Side

1   Always arrive to class on time.

2   Stay for the entire class. Teachers will take notice of those who sneak out early.

3   Turn your phone off or at the very least, put it on silent mode.

4   Never text or answer your phone in class.

5   Ask your teacher in advance if you're planning on recording their lectures. Some do not allow it.

6   Do not try to save time by eating meals in class. In fact, most professors don't tolerate any food or drink apart from water.

7   Contribute to class discussions when appropriate.

8   Stay away from conversation with other students when your teacher is addressing the class.

9   Make sure to address your professor properly. Some teachers have a doctoral degree and therefore have "Dr." before their names. Some teachers take offense when addressed inappropriately. If you're unsure just say "Professor" before their last name.

10   Never pack up early. Give your teacher your 100% undivided attention until the class is over.

The Classroom Checklist

- ☐ Calculator
- ☐ Pen and pencil
- ☐ An extra pen and pencil
- ☐ Whiteout and eraser
- ☐ Post-it flags
- ☐ Index cards
- ☐ Notebook
- ☐ Kleenex

- ☐ Textbooks
- ☐ Tylenol or Advil
- ☐ Highlighters
- ☐ Fully charged laptop
- ☐ Power adapter for laptop
- ☐ Water
- ☐ Backpack to keep it all in

CHAPTER 3

Dorm Room Survival

Moving into your dorm room and need boxes to pack? Go to a local liquor store. They will have tons of boxes that can hold good weight.

The easiest way to make friends quickly in college is to always leave your dorm room door open when you're in the room.

Put old newspapers at the bottom of your trash bin. They will absorb any food juices and make for a cleaner disposal.

Is your shower head not working like it used to? Pour some white vinegar into a plastic bag and secure it to the head with a rubber band. Run the shower for a bit and it'll be good as new.

Put things back where you first looked for them, not where you found them.

Found some ants in your dorm? Forget using all those gross chemicals to kill them. Instead, get a spray bottle, fill it three-quarters full with water and the remaining quarter with salt. Shake well and spray the colony.

Sick of old smelly food containers? Put some crunched up newspaper inside and leave overnight. The paper will absorb the smell by the morning.

Set your dorm room temperature between 60°F and 67°F. This is said to be the best temperature for a good night's sleep.

A coat hanger makes for a perfect kitchen towel holder. Just cut it in the center of the long horizontal part and slide a paper towel roll right through. Use the handles of your kitchen cabinets to hold the hanger up.

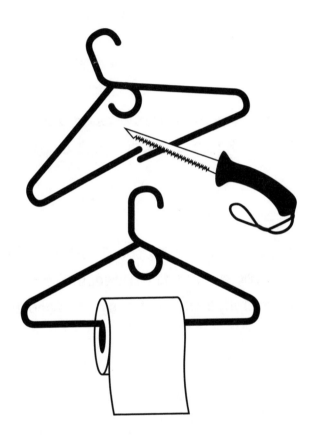

Put Febreze car deodorizers on your air vents to make your room smell amazing!

Drop your nail polish on the floor? Pour some sugar on it. The sugar will immediately clump up the nail polish, making it easy to sweep away.

Get your roommates to try the microwave challenge: While microwaving, see how much of the kitchen you can clean up.

Need to clean your electronic devices? Use a coffee filter. It works like a charm and leaves your screens scratch free.

Put a stocking over a vacuum cleaner to find tiny lost items like earrings.

Feeling homesick? Draw a picture of your favorite comfort food. Seriously! A study showed that people who drew pictures of pizza and cupcakes had up to a 28% positive increase in their moods.

Adding a tablespoon of vanilla extract to a gallon of paint will make your finished dorm room smell like cookies instead of chemicals, and won't affect the color.

When you're finished painting your dorm room, put some of the same paint in a baby food jar for quick touch-ups.

Roommate's phone alarm going off? Call their phone and it will turn it off.

Dorm room a little stinky? Put dry tea bags around your room. They will absorb the unpleasant odor.

Out of clean pillowcases? Use a T-shirt.

Stick pieces of Velcro to the back of your remote and the side of your coffee table. You'll never lose your remote again!

Homemade air freshener: Mix together 2 tablespoons of baking soda, $\frac{1}{8}$ cup of fabric softener, and hot water. Pour it into an empty spray bottle and spritz your room.

10 Unusual Items to Keep in Your Medicine Cabinet

1   Honey.
A teaspoon of honey is great for soothing a sore throat and for curing a hangover.

2   Horseradish.
Mix 1 tablespoon of horseradish with 1 cup of olive oil. Let sit for 30 minutes, then apply as a massage oil to any muscles aching from the flu.

3   Gatorade.
Drinking two glasses of Gatorade can relieve headache pain almost instantly.

4   Toothpaste.
A little bit of toothpaste makes an excellent salve for a burn.

5   Altoids.
These breath fresheners are not only great to pop in right before a date, but they are also a fantastic cure for a stuffy nose.

6   Elmer's multipurpose glue.
       Pour a drop over a splinter, let dry, and peel the dried
       glue along with the splinter right off the skin.

7   White vinegar.
       Soak a cotton ball in white vinegar and apply it to a
       bruised area for 1 hour. This will reduce the blueness
       and speed up the healing process.

8   Quaker oats.
       Mix two cups of oats with one cup of water, microwave
       for 1 minute and apply to any area of the skin causing
       muscle and arthritis pain.

9   Listerine.
       Soaking your toenails in Listerine mouthwash will
       get rid of toenail fungus.

10   Peppermint oil.
       Spiders hate peppermint oil. Put some in a squirt
       bottle, spray the area where you've seen them, and
       watch the spiders run.

Research shows that being continuously sleep-deprived makes you dumb, irritable, distracted, unhappy, and fat. The exact opposite of what you want to be while at school.

Fruit fly problem? Put some fruit or honey in a cup and cover it with plastic wrap. Poke a few holes on top and watch your problem disappear.

Using your phone as an alarm clock? Put it in a glass cup. This will amplify the sound of your alarm and make it a lot harder to sleep through it.

Having trouble sleeping? Try blinking your eyes really fast for a minute. Tired eyes help you fall asleep quicker.

The best way to clean a microwave: Put a cup of hot water mixed with vinegar inside the microwave, turn it on for three to five minutes, and wipe clean with ease.

Make your dorm smell like Christmas by adding a few cinnamon sticks, 4 orange halves, 1 cup of cranberries, and 2 rosemary sprigs into a large pot. Cover the mix with water and let it simmer all day long.

Looking for something? Scan from right to left with your eyes. You'll pick up more since your brain isn't used to reading that way.

Get rid of water stains on your furniture by spreading mayonnaise over the stain and leaving it for 15 minutes. Seems bizarre but it really works!

Use a blow dryer to instantly defog any mirror.

Having a dorm room movie night?
Put your sweatshirt on backward
and use the hood as your own
personal popcorn bowl.

Trying to sneak out at night without your roommates knowing? Lifting up on a door while opening or closing it will often keep it from squeaking and waking people up.

Need a quick repair manual?
On *www.iFixIt.com* you can download the repair manuals for almost anything.

Dorm Room Tip: Buy a plunger before you *need* a plunger.

A bundle of chalk hung in a closet will absorb extra moisture and keep your clothing fresh and dry.

No air conditioning in your dorm? Put a two-liter bottle of frozen water in front of your fan and it'll be like you have your own personal air conditioner.

If you ever want to call a meeting with your roommates, just turn off the Wi-Fi router and wait in the room in which it's located. You'll round up all of your roommates within minutes!

Get rid of any lingering odor by taping
dryer sheets on top of your vents.

You can fix scratched wood by mixing $\frac{1}{2}$ cup
of vinegar and $\frac{1}{2}$ cup of olive oil together
and rubbing it on the scratched surface.

When moving in, pack heavy items, like your books, in a rolling suitcase. Boxes are hard to carry and tend to tear when they're too heavy.

When putting together build-it-yourself furniture, use a muffin tin or ice cube tray to separate all the screws, nails, and fasteners. This will make for easy access during the build.

Add a magnetic strip to your wall and never lose your bobby pins, tweezers, or nail clippers again!

Dorm room too hot and stuffy? Hang a damp towel over an open window. Your place will cool down in a matter of minutes.

The Dorm Room Checklist

☐ Bed sheets and blankets

☐ Pillows and pillowcases

☐ Mattress pad

☐ Foam topper

☐ Mini fridge

☐ Alarm clock

☐ Floor and desk lamps

☐ Calendar

☐ White board and/or bulletin board

☐ Paper clips

☐ Stapler and staples

☐ Trash can

☐ Condoms

☐ iPod dock

☐ Area rug

☐ Wall décor

CHAPTER 4

Things Your Mom Won't Do for You Anymore

Take a picture of the inside of your fridge on your phone before you go grocery shopping. You'll never forget anything at the store again!

Got a stuck zipper? Rub it with the tip of a graphite pencil and it'll work again.

Mom not there to take your splinter out?
Apply a paste of baking soda and water and
wait for the splinter to pop out of the skin.

If you wake up with a sore throat, mix water,
2 tablespoons honey, 2 tablespoons vinegar,
dash of cinnamon, and 2 tablespoons of lemon
juice together. Drink it and you'll feel
better within the hour. Works every time!

6 Ways to Prevent Chronic Headaches

1   Get the right amount of sleep

2   Reduce your stress levels

3   Practice mindfulness-based cognitive therapy

4   Stop chewing gum

5   Improve your posture

6   Try acupuncture

Flattened pillow? Put it in the sun for thirty minutes. The sun will absorb any moisture caught in the pillow and plump it up.

Need to dry your clothes quickly before class? Throw a dry bath towel into the dryer along with your wet clothes. They'll dry much faster.

Something in your eye? Hold your eyelashes and pull your eyelid down with your fingers, then blink rapidly several times.

Get rid of nighttime coughs by putting Vicks VapoRub on your feet and then placing socks over them. Your cough will stop within minutes.

Feeling sick? Eating 10–12 almonds will have the same effect as taking an aspirin.

Get something in your eye?
Pour water into a bowl big enough for your face and open your eyes in it. The irritating object should come right out.

Looking for the best way to fold a T-shirt?
Fold the bottom fourth of your shirt up.
Place the left side of the shirt toward the
center, folding at the shoulder, and do the
same with the right side. Fold the right
sleeve in toward the center so that the left
side is folded neatly. Fold the bottom half of
the shirt up and flip the entire shirt over,
so that the folds are hidden beneath.

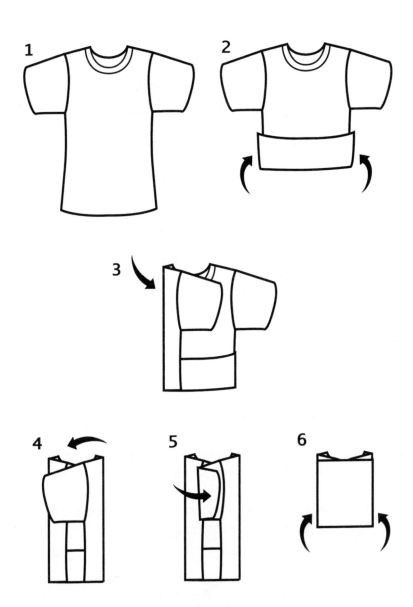

10 Common Stains and How to Remove Them

Vinegar Solution:
$\frac{1}{3}$ cup white vinegar to $\frac{2}{3}$ cup cold water

Detergent Solution:
10 milliliters detergent per $\frac{1}{2}$ liter water

Ammonia Solution:
5% ammonia and 95% cold water

1   BEER: Sponge with white vinegar solution.

2   GREASE: Sponge with dry-cleaning fluid, then sponge with detergent solution. Repeat until stain is gone.

3   INK: Flush with cool water and blot up excess ink. Sponge with vinegar solution.

4   MUD: Let dry, then brush and rinse repeatedly with cold water.

5   PAINT: Sponge with thinner or turpentine until paint disappears; sponge and rinse with water.

6   WINE: Sponge with detergent solution followed by vinegar solution.

7   VOMIT: Put coffee grounds on it first to get rid of the smell and dehydrate it so you can sweep it up. Then sponge the remains with a solution of $\frac{1}{5}$ cup of salt to 1 liter of water.

8   COFFEE: Sponge lightly with dry-cleaning fluid, then sponge with warm water.

9   BLOOD: Sponge with ammonia solution, then with detergent solution.

10   CORDIAL OR JUICE: Get to it fast! Sponge with detergent solution, then with ammonia solution, and finally with vinegar solution.

Gum stuck to your clothes? Boil vinegar and pour it over the gum. Use a brush to wipe off. The gum will come off instantly!

Break something? *www.FixItClub.com* will show you step by step how to fix just about anything.

Something stuck under the fridge? Tape a paper towel roll to your vacuum. You can easily bend and flatten it to reach places!

There are a ton of hiccup remedies out there, but recent studies have shown that the level of CO_2 in your bloodstream is the key. Therefore, breathing into a plastic bag for about 30 seconds should guarantee you relief.

Mom not there to stop your nosebleed?
Put cotton on your upper gums right behind
the small dent below your nose and press
against it hard. This cartilage is where most
of the blood comes from.

To cure a sore throat, add a teaspoon of
honey to Jell-O mix and heat it up. The
gelatin will coat and soothe your throat.

An old CD spindle makes for the perfect bagel holder. They are great for packing school lunches.

Need a better grip on something like a jar, hammer, or screwdriver? Wrap a few rubber bands around it.

What those weird looking laundry symbols on your clothes mean.

Laundry Symbols Guide

TUMBLE DRY · DO NOT TUMBLE DRY · HANG DRY · DRY FLAT

HIGH HEAT · WARM HEAT · DO NOT IRON · DRY CLEAN · DO NOT DRY CLEAN

HAND WASH · NORMAL WASH · GENTLE WASH · BLEACH · DO NOT BLEACH

Out of toilet cleaner?
Pop a couple Alka-Seltzer tabs in, then come
back in 10 minutes to a nice clean shiny bowl.

Put a small amount of water in a glass when
you microwave your pizza to keep the crust
from getting chewy.

Mom not there to make sure you get up for school in the morning? Your alarm will be more effective at waking you up in the morning if it's the same tone as your ringtone.

Clothes shrink too small? Soak them in a mixture of hot water and hair conditioner for five minutes and then air-dry them.

Feeling nauseated? Smell rubbing alcohol.
It will relieve the nausea almost instantly.

No dryer sheets? Throw in two tinfoil balls
for static-free clothes every time.

Chest congested? Steam a sliced or chopped onion, and stand over the pan while it's heating. The sulfuric acid will break up the mucus and help you breathe better.

Have a bad toothache?
Rub ice on the back of your hand on the v-shaped webbed area between your thumb and index finger. A study showed that this can relieve the pain by up to 50%!

Mom not there to iron your shirt?
Hang it up in the bathroom while you shower.
All the wrinkles will come out by the time
you're done.

Put a used, wet sponge in the microwave for
two minutes to kill 99% of the bacteria in it.

If a shirt or sweater has static cling, put a safety pin in it. The static will instantly go away.

Accidentally get pen or an ink stain on your clothes? Scrub some toothpaste into it, let it dry, and then wash. The stain will disappear.

10 Ways to Make Waking Up Easier

1   Plan or pre-make an exciting breakfast.

2   Put your alarm clock on the other side of the room so you have no choice but to get out of bed.

3   Drink water before going to bed.

4   Turn off your phone so you won't be interrupted or tempted to check it while falling asleep.

5   Get the right amount of sleep according to the human sleep cycle and the time you need to wake up. Sleepyti.me will give you the perfect time to go to bed according to your wakeup time.

6   Sleep in total darkness. Melatonin, the sleep hormone, is produced in the dark, meaning a better, deeper sleep.

7   Read before you go to bed. This makes your eyes tired and tricks your brain into thinking you're tired, making it easier to fall asleep.

8   Choose a blanket that keeps you warm. The best sleep temperature is between 62°F and 70°F.

9   Plan something fun and exciting to do in the morning so you'll have no problem getting up to do it.

10   Stretch before you go to bed. This will relax your muscles and make it easier to find a position to sleep in, giving you a better night's sleep.

Sick of static cling on your clothes? Put a small safety pin over the seam; this will drastically reduce the problem.

Someone drop a beer or wine glass? Get rid of the bigger pieces and then put bread on the rest of it. The bread will pick up even the smallest of shards.

Holding a banana peel over a bruise for 10 to 30 minutes will almost completely remove the bruise's color.

It may sound crazy, but white wine will actually take out a red wine stain.

Mom not around to give you a big hug?
On TheNicestPlaceOnTheInter.net you can
get free virtual hugs and positive messages
from strangers. It's no mom hug but it's
guaranteed to light up your day!

Migraine relief: Soak one or both of your
hands in ice water for as long as you can.
While they're in the water, make fists and
open and close them repeatedly.

If you don't own an ironing board, throw your wrinkled clothes in the dryer with a wet sock for 30 minutes.

Fold your T-shirts and stack them vertically so you can see all of them, saving time and space.

Nail polish remover can easily remove any scuffs or stains from your shoes, making them look almost brand new!

The Temporary Mom Checklist

- ☐ Your favorite comfort blanket
- ☐ Iron
- ☐ Ironing board
- ☐ Dryer sheets
- ☐ Detergent
- ☐ Cleaning supplies
- ☐ Your mom's secret recipes
- ☐ Cooking supplies
- ☐ Fruits and vegetables
- ☐ A friend close by who's always on call for a hug
- ☐ Cans of chicken noodle soup (in case you get sick)
- ☐ Your childhood teddy bear
- ☐ A really loud alarm clock
- ☐ Bottle of multivitamins
- ☐ Hand sanitizer
- ☐ Sunscreen

CHAPTER 5

Homework Hacks

Short a few words on an essay?
You can actually add words to the end of
paragraphs and turn their font to white.
Your professor won't be able to see them and
it will add to your word count!

Need to read a book faster?
Place a piece of your favorite candy on each
paragraph. When you reach each paragraph
you get to eat that piece.

Avoid using the word "very" because it's lazy.
Someone isn't very tired, she is exhausted.
Something is very bad, it's atrocious. Someone
isn't very afraid, he's terrified.

Stumped on a question or math problem?
Lie down. Your thought process is much
faster when you're lying down,
which is why you always lie down at
psychiatrist's appointments.

The easiest way to finish a paper in no time
is to pick a subject that infuriates you.
You'll easily be able to rant about it and the
pages will fly by.

Need a quick and simpler definition of a
word? Use an online thesaurus. They usually
have close to one-word definitions.

Want to write essays and bibliographies like a pro? Get the information from Wikipedia and cite the sources listed at the bottom.

Taking notes with different colored pens kickstarts your visual memory when trying to remember them at another point in time.

Writing something out is the memory
equivalent of reading it seven times. Keep that
in mind when you're getting ready to study.

Didn't finish your paper?
Copy and paste a bunch of random symbols in
a Word document and hand it in.
Your teacher will think the file was
damaged, buying you more time to finish.

Paper due? Low on black ink?
Change the font color to dark tan. It looks
almost identical to black ink.

Playing with puppies and kittens
relieves stress and can help you
perform better on exams.

10 Tips for Pulling an All-Nighter

1   Work at a desk and chair and not a couch, floor, or bed to make sure you avoid falling asleep at all costs.

2   Make sure to work in a well-lit area. Cramming alone in your room with a tiny little lamp on is just asking for you to fall asleep.

3   A big dose of fresh air is a great way to make you feel refreshed and alert.

4   Minimize your distractions. That's right, that means turning your phone off or at least putting it on silent, and refraining from social networks and YouTube videos.

5   Only use coffee and energy drinks as a last resort. If your body is not used to large amounts of caffeine, you may experience a caffeine crash.

6   Take a 10–15-minute break every 60–90 minutes. Make
    sure this includes getting out of your chair to get
    your blood flowing again.

7   Listen to stimulating music in headphones. Classical
    music without lyrics is said to make you more
    productive.

8   Get a study buddy. It's a lot harder to fall asleep when
    you have someone there to smack you every time you
    start nod off.

9   Switch up your tasks and/or subjects. If you have a
    bunch of different things to do, switch from one to
    the other occasionally. This will keep things fresh
    and interesting.

10 Have a 15–20-minute nap just before the sun comes up.
    This will reset your body's internal clock.

Looking for some new music to study to?
Musicovery.com is a site where you can find
new music based on your current mood.

Studying for 30–50 minutes at a time (with
10-minute breaks in between) is the most
effective way to retain information.

Have a paper due? Finding it hard to not get distracted by the Internet? KeepMeOut.com lets you block sites for certain periods of time, so you'll stay focused on the task at hand.

When doing long assignments, set a 30-minute timer and race it. This will prevent you from procrastination.

How to easily convert gallons,
pints, quarts, and cups.

Gallon • Quart • Pint • Cup

You can remember the value of pi (3.1415926) by counting each word's letters in "May I have a large container of coffee?"

Eating chocolate while studying helps the brain retain new information more easily, and has been directly linked to higher test scores.

How to make an essay longer:
Hit CTRL + F and search for "." and change
the font size of the periods from 12 to 14.
They look exactly the same, but will make
your paper significantly longer!

Want to get smarter without realizing it?
Play some Tetris. It's been known to increase
your brainpower by almost 150%.

Take notes on your professor's
ideologies and use them to your advantage
when writing essays.

Believing you have a good memory actually
helps you to have a better memory.

If you can't imagine dropping the mic after
the final sentence in your essay, your
conclusion needs to be stronger.

Effective study technique: Read through a page of your notes once, then try to recall as much of what you read as possible. Do this for every page you need to study until you are happy. Past recollection makes future recalling easier.

Studying in your room? Keep your shoes on. Your mind associates having your shoes on with being busy, so you'll be less distracted.

Chew gum when you're studying, and then chew the same flavor when you take the test. This has been known to improve memory.

Writing papers is a formula. An 8-page paper is roughly 16 paragraphs. If you write an introductory paragraph and a conclusion, that leaves you with 14 body paragraphs left to write. Make a list of 14 arguments that support your thesis, and then rearrange them to make sense chronologically. Once you break them down, papers become a lot easier.

Accidentally type half your essay with caps lock on? In Word, shift + F3 will change anything from caps to no caps and vice versa.

The EasyBib iPhone app will give you a bibliography on any book if you simply scan the barcode.

Leave studying to the very last minute?
Your best chance of passing is to study the
first and last 20% of the syllabus.

Writing an essay? Copy and paste it into
Google translate and have the computer read
it out to you. It'll be much easier to find
errors this way.

How to make your essays longer:

INSTEAD OF THIS	SAY THIS
like	along the lines of
like	in the nature of
in fact	as a matter of fact
always	at all times
now, currently	at present time
now, currently	at this point in time
because	because of the fact that
because	due to the fact that
because	for the reason that
because	in light of the fact that
by	by means of
point out	draw your attention
for	for the purpose of
be able to, can	have the ability to
to	in order to

INSTEAD OF THIS	SAY THIS
on, about	in regard to
although, though	in spite of the fact that
if	in the event that
finally	in the final analysis
about	in the neighborhood of
decide on	make decisions about
when	on the occasion of
twice	on two separate occasions
the water rose	the level of water rose
most	the majority of
the people in	the people who are located in
the pie in	the pie that is included in
until	until such time as
of, on, for, about	with reference to

There is a free website called
www.EssayTyper.com that lets you type a topic
and will write the paper for you in minutes.
Always use this website with caution.

Get a study partner with blue eyes.
Studies show that blue-eyed individuals
study more effectively and tend to perform
better on exams.

The Pomodoro method for
maximum-efficiency studying:
25 minutes of hard work, 5-minute break, and
every third break should be 20 minutes long.

Want to read faster? Chew gum. This can
double or even triple your reading speed
because it distracts the brain signals from
your eyes, ears, and mouth by giving them
something to focus on.

Need some good music to do homework to? Try video game or movie soundtracks. They're designed specifically to provide background sounds that won't mess with your concentration.

You can get most answers to math assignments online by typing in the name of the textbook and then "answers."

When writing essays, always remember to make sure you mention the opposing point of view.

Need to improve your geography quickly? Buy a world map shower curtain. You'll become an expert in no time!

When studying for finals, put your phone on the other side of the room, or better yet in another room completely. This way your laziness will (one hopes) outweigh your boredom.

One of the best ways to study is to pretend that you're going to have to teach the material.

The All-Nighter Checklist

- ☒ Textbooks

- ☒ Laptop or computer

- ☒ Desk or reading lamp

- ☒ Notebook

- ☒ Pen and pencil

- ☒ Water

- ☒ Coffee maker, filters, and ground coffee

- ☒ Red Bull

- ☒ Ipod or Spotify

- ☒ Headphones (noise-canceling ones, if possible)

- ☒ Alarm clock (in case of a quick power nap)

- ☒ Snacks

- ☒ Gum

CHAPTER 6

How to Be Broke

Starbucks offers an even smaller size than tall called a short. It's cheaper and a much healthier size.

By peeing in the shower, you can save about 1,157 gallons of water a year.

Buying something from Apple?
Add it to your shopping cart but don't buy it
yet. In 7–10 days they'll give you a 15–20%
discount on that item.

When grocery shopping,
the cheapest items will be on the top and
bottom shelves, not at eye level.

Mark July 11th down on your calendar. This is free Slurpee day at 7/11!

American quarters with the year 1965 and older on them are now worth $4.20 and their value will only go up!

Put a binder clip at the end of your
toothpaste tube to get every last bit.

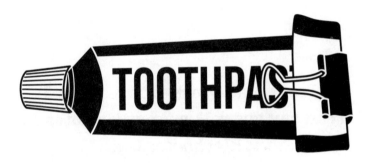

By using the promo code "9ANY,"
you can get any pizza you want at
Pizza Hut for $9 when you order online.

Need some extra cash this semester?
You can buy and sell your study notes on
www.Flashnotes.com.

Never go to the grocery store hungry.
You'll end up buying several things you
don't actually need.

Thinking about getting a new laptop, phone,
or other electronic device for school? Try
holding off on buying it until October.
You can usually get up to 40% off most
electronics during this month.

Grabbing a quick snack from the vending machine but it got stuck? Don't buy the same bag again to unjam it, buy the item above it.

If a Duracell battery leaks and destroys one of your devices, the company will replace the device if it's sent to them with the defective batteries still in place.

Worried about student loans?
www.SponsorChange.org is an organization
that will help you pay off your student
loans in exchange for volunteer work!

If you have a *.edu* e-mail address, you can get
a free Amazon Prime account. This lets you
watch many TV shows and movies via Amazon.

On September 19th you can get a free Krispy Kreme doughnut for talking like a pirate, and get a free dozen if you dress like one too!

Don't buy new ink cartridges for your printer. Take the old ones to Costco and get them filled for only $10.

Too old to trick or treat on Halloween but still want some free stuff? Head over to IHOP and get some free pancakes. You can also get 50-cent corn dogs at Sonic.

When buying something from Craigslist, use a fake e-mail address to lowball the seller by a lot. Then, using your regular e-mail address, offer a reasonable but still lower price. People will usually go for the second offer.

Get free pizza for life: On the back of a

Sbarro's pizza receipt there is a survey that,

when completed, gets you a code for a free

slice of pizza. When you get that pizza you

also get another receipt with the same offer.

Eat and repeat!

Don't pay to learn a new language! You can learn Spanish, French, Italian, German, and Portuguese for free on *www.Duolingo.com.*

Buying a gym membership for the semester? Most times, your health insurance company will completely reimburse the cost for you.

The Ultimate Student Discount List

Food and Drink

- Subway: 10% off
- Chipotle: Free drink
- Burger King: 10% off
- Waffle House: 10% off
- Chick-Fil-A: Free drink
- McDonald's: 10% off
- Pizza Hut: 10–20% off
- IHOP: 10% off
- Dairy Queen: 10% off
- Papa John's: 10–20% off

Apparel and Retail

- J. Crew: 15% off
- Madewell: 15% off
- Urban Outfitters: 10% off
- Banana Republic: 15% off
- Goodwill: Most locations will give you 10% off
- Topshop: 10% off
- Ralph Lauren: 10% off
- Levi's: 15% off online orders to students studying in the United States only

Electronics

- Amazon: The student program is free to join and includes six months of free two-day shipping as well as e-mail alerts.
- Apple: Apple offers a different back-to-school student discount each year on computers, iPads, and iPhones.
- Sony: The Sony Education Store allows students to save up to 10% at checkout.
- Adobe: Save as much as 60% off the retail price of all of their popular programs.

- Inkjet Willy: Save 10% on printer ink and toner with the coupon code WILLY10.
- HP: Save on weekly featured PCs and tablets with savings of 10–20% off, plus free shipping.

Entertainment

- AMC Theatres: Discounted movie tickets on Thursday nights.
- Cinemark Theatres: Discounted movie tickets with valid student ID.
- New York Mets: $10 tickets with a valid student ID.
- Carnegie Hall: Tickets for $10 at the box office only. Eligible performances are announced up to two weeks in advance.
- CorePower Yoga: Up to 25% off passes and drop-in classes.

Other

- Sam's Club: Discounted membership, plus a $15 gift card.
- FedEx: 20–30% off shipping.
- The *New York Times*: 50% off subscriptions and 75% off the *Wall Street Journal*.
- Greyhound: Up to 50% off on selected routes.
- Geico: Full-time students under 25 can get up to $200 off insurance when they maintain a B average or better.
- Chevrolet: Preferred pricing to students and recent grads on most of their vehicles.

Want to learn more while you're at school?
On *www.Coursera.org* you can take hundreds
of free online courses on any topic from
legit schools all around the world.

Need some extra cash? On *www.Rover.com* you
can sign up to be a dog sitter. Simply look
after someone's dog from your college campus
area and get paid for it!

When buying school supplies online, search for promo codes on Google before making a purchase. You can usually find a variety of discounts from free shipping to 25% off.

Android users: After purchasing an app from Google Play, you can try it out for 2 hours and return it for a refund if you're not satisfied with it.

How to make your own glasses from old beer bottles:

1   Tie a string around the beer bottle, right below its neck.

2   Slip off the string and soak it in lighter fluid.

3   Place the string back around the bottle and light the string with a lighter. Blow out the flame once it's gone all the way around the bottle.

4   Rinse the bottle with cold water. The neck and body of the bottle should separate.

5   Carefully sand the top of your new glass with sandpaper.

6   Drink the night away with your new glass!

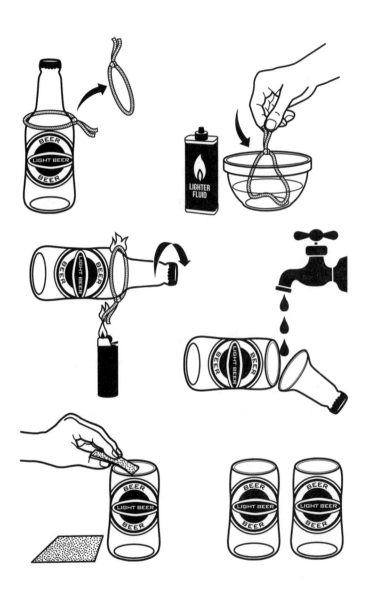

Always order Papa John's Pizza online.
The code 25OFF works every time for
25% off your order!

Want to save money on your food bills?
Drink more water. 75% of Americans are
chronically dehydrated, which makes them
feel hungry when they really aren't.

Want to find cheap eBay auctions? On FatFingers.com you can search what you're looking for and it will send you to similar auctions with incorrect spellings, like "digital canera" or "elecric guitar." Since no one searches for these incorrect spellings, there should be few to no bids for them.

Use ketchup packets as ice packs.
They're the perfect size for small bumps and
bruises and they stay soft enough to form
around any body part.

On the bottom of every Krispy Kreme receipt
is a plea to fill out a survey. You get a free
doughnut for doing the survey. When you get
your doughnut, you get another receipt, with
another survey. Free doughnuts for life!

Want to save money on your utility bill? Put a brick in your top toilet tank. You'll save a brick's worth of water every time you flush the toilet.

Get your first Redbox movie rental for free! Just type in "dvdonme" when it asks for a promo code.

Finding it hard to balance your schoolwork and your workout schedule?
Download the app Pact for some extra motivation, and cash! The app has a community of users that will literally pay you to stick to your workout schedule.

Grocery stores stack their products by sell-by date, which means the oldest food is in the front. Make sure to always grab food from the back.

For frequent Starbucks customers: Buy and use a membership card. It only takes five transactions to get to the green level, and then coffee and tea refills are free.

Want a cheap Xbox/PS4 for your dorm room?
Check out Craigslist around the time report
cards get sent home.

When buying from a vending machine, insert
your lowest-value coin first. If the machine
isn't working, you won't lose that much money.

10 Sites to Get
Free Textbooks From

1   *BookBoon.com*

2   *eBookee.org*

3   *ManyBooks.net*

4   *FeedUrBrain.com*

5   *FlatWorldKnowledge.com*

6   *2020ok.com*

7   *FreeTextBooks.com*

8   *Gutenberg.org*

9   *wikibooks.org*

10   *En.Bookfi.org*

Get one last bowl of cereal from your box by sifting the remnants through a kitchen strainer.

Hate paying ridiculous prices for college textbooks? The Swappet app allows you to buy used textbooks at a fraction of the price, along with selling your old ones.

Are you close with your off-campus neighbors?
Share your Wi-Fi and split the bill.

Download the Apple free app of the week even
if you don't need it. You can delete it and
re-download it whenever you want for free!

The Broke College Student Checklist

- ☐ Ramen noodles

- ☐ Generic condiments

- ☐ Gmail account (for making free long-distance calls)

- ☐ A piggy bank

- ☐ Natural Ice and/or Rubinoff

- ☐ A weekly/monthly/yearly budget

- ☐ Credit card

- ☐ Microwavable meals

- ☐ PB&J sandwiches

- ☐ Travel-size toiletries

- ☐ Tissues to wipe away your broke tears

CHAPTER 7

Party Hacks

Buy your alcohol at Costco or Sam's Club.

You don't need a membership and it's

usually 25–35% off. It's great for when

you're hosting a party, but keep in mind

that you may have to do a little persuading

with the card-checker employees if they're

unaware of this policy.

Four words to get free alcohol at a party:
"I've never been drunk."

Holding your drink at bellybutton level at bars/parties has been proven to make you look more confident.

Stuck chatting up a mumbler at a party? Lean in with your right ear. It's better than your left at following the rapid rhythms of speech.

Tilting your head to the right and slightly up makes you look more attractive. Tilting it to the right makes you look more intelligent.

Women are more influenced by how a man
smells than how he looks.
Men, choose your fragrance wisely.

Hide your beer in a soft drink cup. Keep ice
at the bottom to keep it cool and put the
straw through the top. No one will ever know
the difference!

How to open a beer
with a piece of paper:

1   Fold a square piece of paper in half, turning it into a
     rectangle. Now fold it in half again to form a square.

2   Fold the paper in half a few times until you have a
     long, thick rectangle.

3   Fold the rectangle in half once so that the right end
     is now touching the left end.

4   Hold the ends of the paper with one hand. Place the
     folded edge underneath the cap and press upward to
     open the bottle.

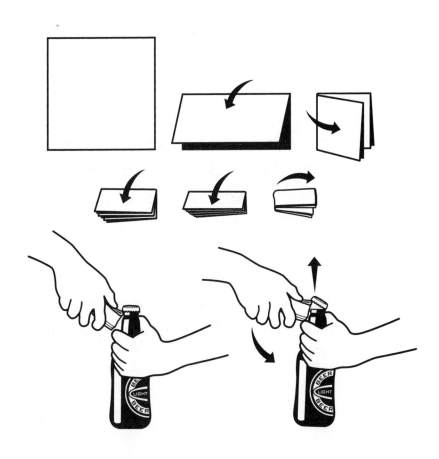

Psychologists say that when meeting someone for the first time, you only have about 7 seconds to make a powerful first impression. So make it count!

If you're drunk and have the urge to vomit, taking short, rapid breaths can help it go away.

Put glow sticks in a cooler for easy drink grabbing without needing a flashlight.

Not sure if someone is interested in you? Look at their eyes. People's pupils expand by about 45% when looking at a love interest.

When you meet someone for the first time at a party, skip awkward introductions by asking things like "What's new with you?"

Ways to Cure a Hangover

1   Try honey on crackers. The fructose in the honey will help flush out the alcohol in your system.

2   Believe it or not, soaking your feet in hot water will help your head feel better.

3   Drink sports drinks. They always have excellent hydrating agents in them.

4   Eat a big, greasy meal before you start drinking. Grease lines your stomach and prepares it for the night's battle.

5   Drink one glass of water for every alcoholic drink you have and you'll get drunk without getting a hangover.

6   Eat some toast. Toast will bring your blood sugar levels back up to normal after a hard night on your liver.

7   Drink lighter beer. The darker the color of the alcohol you're drinking, the worse your hangover will be.

8   Go for a walk, run, or swim. Although it may not be fun at first, it will release endorphins and improve your mood.

9   Drink water with an Alka-Seltzer. They even have a Morning Relief formula specifically designed for hangovers.

10   Bananas help relieve headaches, depression, and cramps. Perfect for a hangover!

11   Drink Pedialyte, a children's medicine. It's designed to replenish and rehydrate your body with electrolytes and has been known to work wonders. It also comes in an ice pop form if you want a cure and a treat.

Mixing alcohol with Diet Coke will get you drunker than if you mix it with regular Coke.

Dent in your beer pong ball? Hold a lighter under it (not too close) and watch the gasses expand the dent outward, making it good as new.

You can also fix multiple beer pong balls at once by boiling a pot of water and throwing them in for about 10 seconds.

You can make cheap wine taste AMAZING by putting it in a blender for 20 seconds. This softens the tannins in the wine and is a quick way to aerate it.

Those lines on red Solo cups are
actually alcohol measurements.

12 ounces
Beer

5 ounces
Wine

1 ounce
Liquor

Suspect someone is giving you the wrong phone number? Read it back to them incorrectly, and if they correct you, it's legit.

Never take ibuprofen on an empty stomach to cure a hangover. It can actually tear your stomach lining.

Stop telling people what's in the cooler and just cut off the labels and tape them to the lid.

Ladies: Want to know if a guy is into you? Pay attention to his voice. Men tend to lower their voices when they are talking to someone they are interested in.

Feel the urge to vomit?
You can stop yourself by eating a mint
or chewing minty gum.

If you tend to wake up early after a night
of drinking, it might be because your blood
sugar is low. A slice of bread with peanut
butter can solve this.

Flip a pizza box around on your lap so when opened the lid covers your chest. You now have made yourself a pizza bib!

The colors you wear account for 62–90% of someone's first impression. People who wear brighter colors tend to do better.

Always buy the first pitcher or round of drinks. You'd be surprised how long you can drink on the phrase "I bought the first one."

Man hack: Wearing a red shirt makes women find you more attractive. Many studies have shown that women are culturally and biologically attracted to men wearing red.

A quick and easy iPhone speaker using a toilet paper roll:

1   Using scissors cut a small, iPhone-sized slit into the top of a toilet paper roll.

2   Add tacks to the bottom of the roll, so that it stands up on its own. Insert your iPhone into the slit.

3   Turn up the music and enjoy!

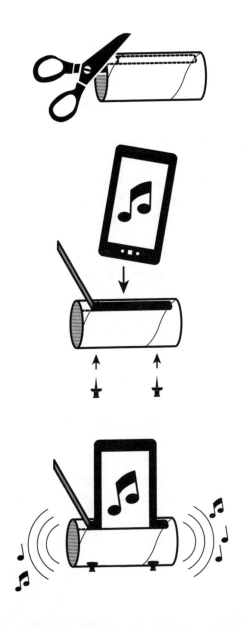

10 Tips to Become a Beer Pong Champion

1 Before you throw, always get the ball wet. A dry ball will float around more, and has a bigger chance of slipping out of your hands.

2 Standing in the right position is key. Whichever hand you shoot with, that foot is in front. The opposite is farther back.

3 Grip the beer pong ball with only your thumb and middle finger. This allows you to have a way more consistent throw from turn to turn.

4 Bouncing can win and lose you games. Getting a bounce shot in counts as two cups, so always be on the lookout for when your opponent is not looking. On the flip side, as distracting as your surroundings may be, always be on the lookout for your opponent trying to sneak in a bounce shot. You're allowed to block bounce shots.

5   Pretend like you're not paying attention. Then when
     the opposing team sees you, they will try for a bounce
     shot, and you can easily block their pathetic attempt.

6   Get good at throwing with your nondominant hand.
     Doing this will allow you to have a great advantage
     when it comes to doing trick shots.

7   Go for the glory. If your opponent is drinking from a
     red cup and you shoot it into their cup, it's game over.
     You win!

8   Aim for a specific part of the cup, not just the cup in
     general. This will give you a greater advantage than
     people who just aim for the entire thing.

9   Use your legs. As you throw use your legs to thrust
     upward, like the motion you would use to throw a
     basketball.

10   Drink a beer before the game. The perfect throw never
     comes from the nervous guy whose heart is racing 100
     miles a minute. Relax and have a drink.

When throwing a punch, and I hope you never have to, clench your fist only at the last second. You lose a lot of power clenching throughout the swing.

Last longer in the sack: Taking longer, deeper breaths will relax you and your heart rate, and allow you to have more control over your arousal level.

Don't want people in class to see a hickey
you got last night? Place a cold spoon
on it for a few minutes.

Drinking game: Shot Roulette. Spin the bottle
and take the shot you get. Make sure that not
all of the shots are alcoholic. Expert level:
Play with glasses you can't see through.

Mix vodka and gummy candies in a container and wait a day. Then get drunk while snacking!

Want to make a bottle of beer cold really fast? Wrap it in a wet paper towel and put it in the freezer for two minutes.

If you feel like you're going to vomit,
start humming. It's nearly impossible
to gag while humming.

On New Year's Eve, from 6 P.M. to 6 A.M.,
AAA will tow drunk you and your car back to
your place for free.

How to Open a Beer
with Another Beer:

1   In each hand, hold the neck of each beer. Take the beer
    in your right hand and flip it over so that the cap can
    fit snugly underneath the cap of the beer in your left
    hand.

2   Gently press up into the left-hand cap with the beer in
    your right hand. This should open that beer.

3   Now, take the open beer and place it on the table.
    Place the cap of the unopened beer on top of the opened
    beer's rim and press down on it with your free hand.

4   Share your extra beer with a friend or double fist like
    a pro!

Trying to identify a song at a party? Lean in with your left ear. It's better than your right at picking up music tones.

Look at someone's elbow when you high-five. You'll never miss again.

5 Quick Drinking Tips

1   Pour your own drinks.

2   Have a cup of water between every drink.

3   Don't be that loud drunk who gets the party shut down.

4   Stick to one kind of alcohol throughout the night.

5   If your friend is in really bad shape don't hesitate to call 911 or 311 (non-emergency). Don't be that person who thinks someone can sleep it off.

Don't know anyone at the party? Keep in
mind that it's better to be interested in
other people than to try to be interesting.
Mimicking the body language of the person
you're talking to subconsciously makes them
more receptive to you.

You can clear a room full of cigarette smoke in about a minute by spinning a wet towel around.

Feeling dizzy in bed from drinking too much? Put one of your legs on the ground. It will make your body feel more stable, and reduce that spinning feeling.

The Party Animal Checklist

☐ Ping pong balls

☐ Red solo cups

☐ Shot glasses

☐ Cooler

☐ Ice

☐ Mixers and chasers

☐ Snacks

☐ Speakers

☐ An awesome playlist

☐ Beer

☐ Beer

☐ Beer

CHAPTER 8

Food and Nutrition

When heating leftovers, space out a circle in the middle of the food. The empty space will help your food heat up much more evenly.

Have leftover coffee from the morning? Use it to make coffee ice cubes, which will cool down your coffee without diluting it.

Nutella mug cake: Mix 4 tablespoons flour, $\frac{1}{4}$ teaspoon baking powder, $\frac{1}{4}$ cup Nutella, and 3 tablespoons milk. Microwave for 1 minute.

Open your bag of chips from the bottom since most of the flavoring has sunk there.

Microwave two big bowls at the same time by elevating the second bowl with a mug or another small, microwave-safe container.

10 Metabolism Boosters That Can Prevent the Freshman 15

1 Almonds

2 Spinach

3 Cold water

4 Turkey

5 Salmon

6 Hot peppers

7 Coffee

8 Ginger

9 Yogurt

10 Green tea

When it comes to staying awake, apples are actually more powerful than caffeine.

Always feel tired even after getting a good, long sleep? You're probably dehydrated— drink some water right when you wake up.

Break off the end of a
department store pants hanger for
the perfect chip bag clamp.

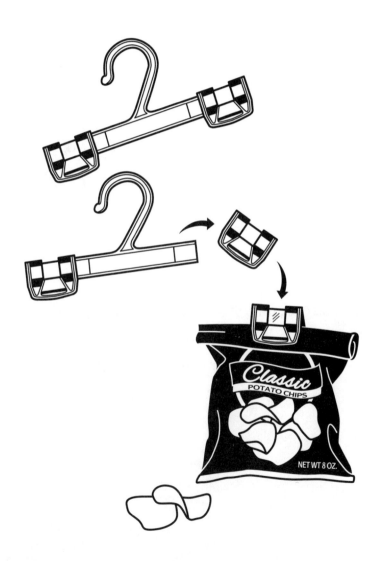

Run your bacon under cold water before cooking it. Doing so will reduce shrinkage by up to 50%.

You can order Starbucks drinks at "kid's temperature." The drink will be much cooler and you'll never burn your tongue again!

Sick of all those broken spaghetti noodles? An old Pringles can will fit your pasta perfectly.

Homemade Wendy's Frosty:
Blend 1 cup unsweetened almond milk, 1 frozen banana, 1 tablespoon cocoa powder, 1 teaspoon vanilla, $\frac{1}{2}$ teaspoon chia seeds, and 8–10 ice cubes. Enjoy!

Hate when your Hot Pocket explodes
in the microwave? Stab it with a fork
before you put it in.

Instantly improve your diet by eliminating
any foods that have a mascot.

Want x-ray vision? Well, I can't help there, but kiwi fruit contains lutein, an antioxidant that can actually help improve your eyesight.

Have a particularly stressful class? Eat a banana before it. They are known as a happy fruit. Eating just one can help relieve irritable emotions, anger, and/or depression.

The best way to serve pizza at a party:

1   Open the pizza box.

2   Separate the lid of the pizza box from the pizza tray.

3   Cut the pizza box lid in half.

4   Cut the lid in half again and serve pizza slices on each of the four lids.

5   Save half of the pizza for later by folding the tray in half.

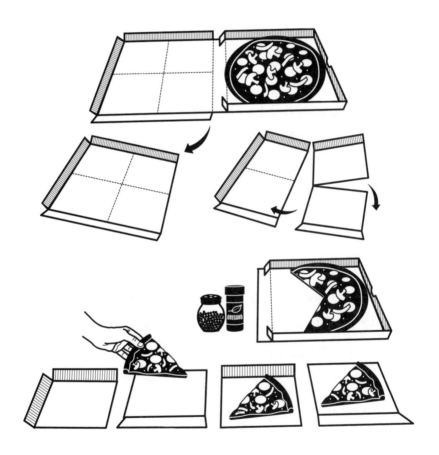

If you accidentally over-salt your food while it's still cooking, drop in a peeled potato. It will absorb the excess salt for an instant fix.

When you want to put a two-liter bottle of soda away, shake it up a little bit first. It will stay fizzy for weeks.

Want to make the best hot chocolate known to man? Try warming up milk with Nutella.

The smell of an orange relieves stress. Smelling an orange or eating one can reduce stress by over 70%.

10 Starbucks Secret Menu Items

1   Captain Crunch: Strawberries and Creme Frappucino with a pump of caramel, two pumps of toffee, one pump of hazelnut, and two scoops of chocolate chips.

2   Neopolitan Frappucino: Ask for a Strawberries and Creme Frappucino with some vanilla bean powder and a pump of mocha.

3   Raspberry Cheesecake: Order a White Chocolate Mocha (iced, hot, or as a Frappucino) and add a few pumps of raspberry.

4   Chocolate Turtle Flavor: Any drink that contains mocha, caramel, and toffee nut.

5   Oreo Frappucino: Ask for a Double Chocolate Chip Frappucino with white mocha syrup instead of the regular mocha.

6 The Nutella: Order a Cafe Misto with a pump of chocolate, a pump of hazelnut, and caramel drizzle.

7 Biscotti Frappucino: Buy a biscotti and ask the barista to blend it up with your favorite flavor of Frappucino. It blends nicely and adds a great crunch to any frozen coffee.

8 Cotton Candy Frappucino: Order a Vanilla Bean Frappucino and add raspberry syrup. Ask for 1 pump for a tall, 1.5 pumps for grande, and 2 pumps for venti.

9 French Vanilla Flavor: Any drink that has half toffee nut and half vanilla.

10 Year-round Pumpkin Spice Latte: Order a latte with a pump of chai and a pump of white chocolate mocha.

Make "cookie bowls" by simply turning your muffin or cupcake pan upside down, and putting cookie batter over top to bake.

Roommate using the kitchen? Throw some hot dogs or ramen noodles in your coffee pot with water and turn it on. They'll both be ready to eat within 10 minutes.

Butter too hard or frozen to spread? Grab a cheese grater and grate it right onto the bread. Works like a charm!

If you peel a banana from the bottom, you won't have to pick the little stringy things off of it.

When reheating rice or pasta in the microwave, sprinkle a little bit of water on top first. This will make it taste way better, almost like you just made it.

The easiest and fastest way to make grilled cheese:

1   Flip your toaster on its side.

2   Place slices of bread in each toaster slot. Top the bread with your favorite kind of cheese.

3   Toast until cheese is melted, and sandwich the two slices of bread together with the cheese in the middle.

The Best Times to Drink Water

- 2 glasses after waking up will help activate your internal organs.

- 1 glass 30 minutes before a meal will help with your digestion.

- 1 glass before taking a bath/shower will help lower your blood pressure.

- 1 glass before going to bed will help you avoid stroke or heart attack.

Tired of jelly soaking through your peanut butter and jelly sandwiches? Spread the peanut butter on both sides of the bread and put the jelly in the middle.

By drinking black coffee in the morning before class you'll not only save calories, but you will also jump-start your digestive system for the school day.

Don't have any butter for your grilled cheese? Whisk an egg until fully mixed, then spread it with a fork onto your bread before placing it on the pan.

Six foods that have been shown to improve your mood: Oatmeal, cereal, salmon, milk, dark chocolate, and bananas.

Trying to stay awake in class?
Chewing cinnamon-flavored gum will keep
you awake and alert.

Cheesy ramen: Pour boiling water on noodles,
stir, then strain. Add $\frac{1}{4}$ cup of cheese and $\frac{1}{4}$
cup of milk. Stir to mix and enjoy!

Eating grapes improves the brain's ability to process new information and thus enhances your intelligence.

Use a recycled Mio bottle for salad dressing, soy sauce, and more. Peel off the label, pop off the top and fill. It's a great size to put in your lunch box for extra sauce, and it doesn't leak!

Too lazy to do the dishes?
Use a tortilla as a plate. No dishes needed,
plus you get to eat it after.

Put pancake mix in an empty ketchup bottle
for a clean, no-mess experience.

Turn any bag of chips into an instant snack bowl:

1   Grab a bag of your favorite snack.

2   Open the bag.

3   Roll the bottom corners into the bag.

4   Keep rolling in the corners.

5   Roll the corners in some more until the bottom of the bag is flat.

6   Place the bag on a table or solid surface. It should be able to stand on its own.

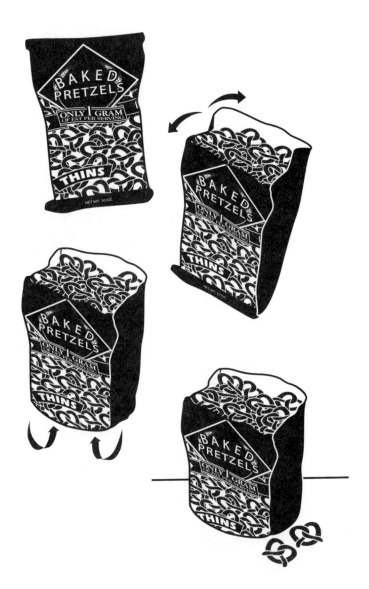

Put crushed up Oreos or Doritos in an old pepper shaker to spice up your bland meals.

Popcorn actually pops better when it's stored in cold places like the refrigerator.

One of the best breakfast foods you can have before exam day is oatmeal. It is a slow-digesting food, which provides a sustained flow of glucose to the brain.

10 Foods for Optimal Brain Function

1   Berries: Slow down the brain's aging process.

2   Hemp seeds: Help your central nervous system.

3   Asparagus: Helps improves cognitive function.

4   Carrots: Reduce cognitive decline.

5   Avocados: Boost your memory and learning capabilities.

6   Dark leafy greens: Enhance brain function.

7   Bananas: Help keep you calm and alert.

8   Watermelon: Keeps your memory sharp.

9   Fish: Helps keep your brain neurons functioning properly.

10   Red wine: Reduces your risk of getting Alzheimer's.

The Starbucks cold beverage lids are
actually designed to be used as coasters!

Friend got the blues? Make a package of
Cookie Dough Oreos by replacing the cream
filling of Oreos with cookie dough.
Your pal will instantly feel better.

PMS SOS smoothie:
Mix together 6 ounces fat-free milk,
1 tablespoon chocolate syrup, ½ banana,
½ cup strawberries, and 1 peeled kiwi.
Add ice, blend, and enjoy.

Unload a fridge pack of Coke in a jiffy by
opening both ends and pulling out the box.

Want to cut a watermelon open without a knife? Take a quarter, make a small incision at the center of the watermelon, and karate chop it in half. No joke, it actually works!

The Kitchen Checklist

- ☐ Plates and bowls
- ☐ Cups and mugs
- ☐ Eating utensils
- ☐ Coffee maker
- ☐ Microwave
- ☐ Toaster
- ☐ Can opener
- ☐ Travel mug
- ☐ Water pitcher
- ☐ Measuring cups
- ☐ Condiments

- ☐ Dish detergent
- ☐ Dish towels
- ☐ Pizza cutter
- ☐ Plastic food containers
- ☐ Ziploc bags
- ☐ Paper towels
- ☐ Bulk snacks and drinks
- ☐ Strainer
- ☐ Dish sponge
- ☐ Chip clips
- ☐ Trash bags

CHAPTER 9

How to Not Be Lazy

Being in a green setting or even glancing at the color green can make you more creative.

Talking to yourself may seem crazy, but it can actually lead to increased behavioral performance, better task performance, and can make you feel better about yourself. But only if you use the 2nd person (you/your).

Try the Sleep Cycle app for the iPhone. This bio—alarm clock measures your sleep cycle and wakes you up at the lightest point in your sleep, which means no more groggy mornings!

Studies show that having plants where you study/do homework can help you think more clearly and recall more information. This is due to the fact that our brains benefit from the exposure to nature.

Sitting on a medicine ball instead of a chair while doing homework can improve your focus and productivity by 50%.

The 80/20 rule: 20 percent of your day produces 80 percent of your results, so by minimizing things that don't matter as much in your school day, you will maximize your overall productivity.

Music with a strong beat stimulates brain waves, which improves human concentration even after you've stopped listening.

Simple breathing technique that helps you regain focus: Breathe in while counting to 3, breathe out while counting to 4.

Play a game on your phone for 3 minutes right after you wake up. This will prepare your mind for the school day and make getting up much easier.

Need to remember to take something with you when you leave the house in the morning? Put it in your shoe so you can't leave without it.

The average person will spend 13.6 years of their life watching television. Imagine the things you could accomplish just by cutting that in half!

Declutter your work space.
A tidy desk equals a tidy mind.

5 Kinds of Naps for Any Occasion

1   The Power Nap (10–20 Minutes): Good for a quick pick-me-up and getting straight back to work.

2   The NASA Nap (26 Minutes): Best before tackling a pile of homework after a long day at school, and was proven by scientists to improve pilot performance by 34% and alertness by 54%.

3   The Bad Nap (30 Minutes): This nap is so common but should be avoided due to the fact that it causes sleep inertia, also known as that groggy sleep hangover.

4   The Slow-Wave (60 Minutes): Helps promote cognitive memory processing. Best before a big presentation, meeting, or interview.

5   The Full Sleep Cycle (90 Minutes): Good for creativity, emotional memory, and procedural memory. Best before a project deadline or a big test/exam.

It may sound absurd but looking at pictures of cute baby animals has been proven to increase concentration and productivity by up to 44%.

Measure the length of your hand from the end of your palm to the top of your middle finger. Memorize that number. Now you can judge the size of anything without a ruler.

Need some motivation? Take a shower. Being clean is proven to increase your productivity.

One of the most valuable things you can learn to do while at school is to say "no" without explaining yourself.

Listening to music for at least 10 minutes each day strengthens your mind's ability to handle stress.

You're more likely to stay focused on your schoolwork while working in a blue room.

Ignore your e-mails, unfinished homework, and last-minute studying when you first wake up in the morning. Your morning foreshadows your whole day, so spend it getting a good breakfast, reading the news, meditating, or working out. You'll be much more productive for the rest of the day.

By ditching the car and taking public transit to school, your mind and hands will be free to get things done on your commute.

Tape some thumbtacks to your snooze button and you'll never be late for your 8 A.M. class again.

Not in the mood to do a project that's due tomorrow? Force yourself to start it. By doing this you can quickly get into the groove of things, and that groove can last hours.

Telling people your goals will push you toward achieving them due to the fact that you will be held accountable for your results.

It's been proven that peppermint stimulates brain activity and makes you concentrate better.

Think positively. Positivity, especially in the future tense, speeds up the creation of cells and reduces stress and anxiety, which actually kill brain neurons.

Singing in the shower daily can help boost your immunity, lower blood pressure, reduce stress, and improve your mood.

Get stuck in a traffic jam on the way to class? Pay attention to which lane the 18 wheelers are using. They have radios and usually let one another know which lanes to avoid.

It's been proven that lying on your right side will help you fall asleep faster than lying on your left.

Never hesitate to take breaks. You can't always be working at 100%. Instead, try to work in shorter bursts.

Make a "leave the dorm" mixtape. Plan a playlist according to the amount of time it takes for you to get ready in the morning. That way when the last song comes on you'll know it's almost time to go.

10 Simple Ways to Defeat Laziness

---

1   Visualize your end product before starting something.

2   Break your tasks into smaller tasks.

3   Make a routine out of your diet and plan meals ahead of time.

4   Think of laziness as a battle; successful people do not let laziness win.

5   Set up a daily routine.

6   Repeat affirmations like "I can accomplish my goal" and "I won't let laziness win."

7   Treat your time like money.

8   Exercise daily.

9   Get the right amount of sleep.

10   Focus on doing one task at a time.

Pick a study partner who is 100% focused. Nothing will stop you from procrastinating better than looking over at a partner who is completely focused on the work.

Always do your least favorite task of the day first thing in the morning. Simply knowing you've completed your most dreaded task will make you much more productive for the rest of the day.

Hitting snooze on your alarm can make you more tired than if you had gotten up right away.

The Two-Minute Rule: If you see something that needs doing and it can be completed within two minutes, do it immediately.

Have a long lecture you have to watch on YouTube? Go to settings and opt for the 2x speed. It will sound a little funny at first but you can easily understand what is said and watch it in half the time!

Your location and surroundings are everything when it comes to being productive. Experiment with doing your schoolwork in a few different places like your dorm room, library, and local coffee shop, and see what works best for you.

If you brush your teeth (and do other small tasks) with the wrong hand you force the brain to work differently.
Your self-control will improve.

Research shows writing goals down will significantly improve your optimism (even six months later), and raise your success rates significantly.

Being surrounded by the color yellow helps you stay focused. Yellow decreases the production of melatonin, a hormone that makes you sleepy.

Color the top edge of your Post-it notes with a marker so you'll always know which side is the sticky. This means no more accidental upside-down or sideways notes.

The Organization Checklist

- ☐ Underbed storage
- ☐ Storage bins
- ☐ Hamper
- ☐ Laundry basket
- ☐ Clothes hangers
- ☐ Coat hooks
- ☐ Shoe rack
- ☐ Closet organizers

- ☐ Drawer organizers
- ☐ Closet rods
- ☐ Vacuum
- ☐ Tool kit
- ☐ Wall mirror
- ☐ Drying rack
- ☐ Shower caddy
- ☐ Bed risers

CHAPTER 10

Other Random Stuff You Should Probably Know

A high GPA looks good on paper,
but networking and building connections
is what gets you a job.

No matter how slowly you progress, you're
still ahead of everyone who isn't trying.

Keep a card with all your emergency contact
numbers and medical information on it in
your wallet. It could save your life someday.

If you want to sound sick when calling in
sick, lie on your back while hanging your
head over the edge of the bed.
You'll sound congested.

Make a password from a goal of yours so
you're constantly reminded of it.

When you talk, you are repeating what you
already know. But if you listen, you may
learn something new.

10 Lessons Almost Every Freshman Learns the Hard Way

1   Always back up your files.

2   Take smart notes. There's nothing worse than trying to study notes that aren't properly formatted and missing some of the major points.

3   Resolve issues with your roommates. Don't let them build to the point where you hate each other.

4   Always set and stick to your budget.

5   The freshman 15 is real.

6   Don't put partying first.

7   Go to every class. You never know when your professor will give crucial test hints or extra credit for attendance.

8   Get a credit card solely to build credit and for emergencies. Keep in mind that this is not free money.

9   Don't drink too much coffee. You can get the same energy from staying hydrated, eating well, and getting enough sleep.

10   Register for classes on time. This can help you avoid having to do an extra semester or summer courses.

The key to confidence is walking into a room and assuming everyone already likes you.

The biggest lie you will tell yourself in college is "I don't need to write that down, I'll remember it."

Finding it hard to meet people at school? Go outside when it's raining with a huge umbrella. You'll meet tons of people in no time!

Can't concentrate on school because you have an annoying song stuck in your head? Sing or listen to the song all the way to the end. People tend to remember unfinished things better; this is called the Zeigarnik effect.

The date rape drug Rohypnol tastes very salty. If your drink suddenly has a salty taste, stop drinking it immediately.

Never keep condoms in your wallet. After
just a month in there, they have a 50%
greater chance of breaking.

Find three hobbies you love:
one to make you money, one to keep you in
shape, and one to be creative.

Wearing headphones does not make your farts silent. Keep this in mind while studying in the library.

When you feel like you need something, but you can't figure out what it is, it's water. It's always water.

In your school bathroom, the stall that is the closest to the door is usually the cleanest because it's the least used.

When meeting people for the first time, try to use their name in conversation. This will establish a sense of trust and friendship right away.

Learning from your mistakes is wise, learning from the mistakes of others is quicker and easier.

Never be afraid to spend a little extra on a new bed and shoes. If you're not in one, you're in the other.

Looking into companies to apply to after you finish school? On *www.GlassDoor.com* you can read real reviews and find out what it's like to work there before you actually do.

Never sleep naked. If there is some kind of emergency in your dorm, it might be too late to put something on.

The easiest way to build up your GPA is to do well at the start of the year when classes and assignments are easier.

Get caught doing something embarrassing on campus? Just say you lost a bet.

If your sleeping pattern is off due to early classes or pulling an all-nighter, try this: Stop eating during the 12–16-hour period before you want to be awake. Once you start eating again, your internal clock will reset, telling your body it's the start of a new day.

Never send your resume to someone as a Word document (unless asked). Send it as a PDF file since it's much cleaner and more professional-looking.

Playing some Frisbee on campus? Use the same arm motion as if you were whipping a towel. This will ensure a straight throw every time.

The best way to get the right answer
on the Internet is not to ask a question, it's
to post the wrong answer.

Don't ever leave a college sports game early.
The most historic games were made in the
final seconds.

10 Little Things That Will Lead to a Happier College Life

1   Drink a lot of water.

2   Get more than 7 hours sleep per night.

3   Wash your face twice a day.

4   Have a bath with Epsom salts.

5   Keep your dorm room clean and organized.

6   Eat fresh fruit.

7   Leave time for yourself.

8   Think positively.

9   Exercise regularly.

10 Listen to music.

The first thing people notice about you,
subconsciously, is your shoes.
Dress to impress.

Want to find a good job after college?
Make friends with as many people in your
field as you can who are on track to graduate
one or two years ahead of you.

Going to bed after 11:30 P.M. on school nights is associated with lower GPA and susceptibility to emotional problems.

Buying school supplies online? Only read the three-star reviews. They're usually the most honest about the pros and cons.

Worried about bombing a job interview? On ThePMInterview.com you can practice a real-life interview with commonly asked questions.

Golden spending rule: If you can't afford two of it, you can't afford it.

Minor in what you love and major in what will get you a job.

The Other Stuff You Might Need for College Checklist

☐ Rechargeable batteries

☐ Extension cords

☐ Scissors

☐ Umbrella

☐ Flashlight

☐ First-aid kit

☐ Duct tape

☐ Bug spray

☐ Snow shovel

☐ Sewing kit

☐ Fan

☐ Bike lock

☐ Ear plugs

☐ Lounging chairs

☐ Light bulbs

☐ Room fragrances

Index

About the Author

Keith Bradford is the sole owner and webmaster of Bradford Media, which publishes 1000LifeHacks.com, YupThatExists.com, and many other blogs/sites. Since its launch at the beginning of 2013, Bradford Media has gained a collective readership of over 500,000, and continues to grow each and every day. He lives just north of Toronto, Canada, in a small suburban town called Aurora, and loves hockey, making music, and reading comic books.